Horse Training

An Exposition On Equine Physical Therapy: A
Comprehensive Manual On Equine Physical Conditioning
And Therapeutic Tools

*(The Comprehensive Guide To Raising And Caring For
Ferghana Horses)*

Manuel Stein

TABLE OF CONTENT

Interesting Details About Your Arabian Horse.......... 1

Getting Along With Your Arab 7

Naturopathic Hair Training 20

Review: Horseback Riding 44

Making Your Thoroughbred Horse Social 69

Practice More..81

Pre-Purchase Interviewing Using The T.R.A.I.L.S. Method 94

Educating Your Foal To Take Charge........................ 107

Interesting Details About Your Arabian Horse

Arabs are lovable creatures by nature who want to satisfy their owners.

One of the earliest horse breeds in the world that humans developed is the Arabian.

Arabian Peninsula rock art and inscriptions from 3500 years ago depicted horses with Arab characteristics.

Around 4,000–5,000 years ago, the Bedouin inhabitants of the Arabian Peninsula may have domesticated the proto-Arabian horse after learning to use the camel. Arabs were bred to be battle horses with intelligence, speed, endurance, and soundness.

Illnesses in Your Arab

Although numerous things can happen even before the age of 20, the majority of health issues will manifest beyond that age. There are four recognised genetic disorders in Arabian horses, and they typically cause the diseased animal to die or be put to sleep.

A test is available for severe combined immunodeficiency disorder (SCID).

Cerebellar Abiotrophy (CA) (offered as an indirect marker test)

Syndrome of Lavender Foals (LFS) (test available)

Malformation of the occipital atlantoaxial (OAAM) (test not yet available)

Tests are currently unavailable for two other conditions: juvenile epilepsy syndrome (JES) and guttural pouch tympany (GPT), the latter of which can affect dogs of different breeds.

Additional requirements for Arabs
Tetanus (Distemper) Strokes
Influenza
Equine encephalomyelitis and rhino pneumonitis
rabies
Worms in the stomach
Laminitis Colic

Sadly, there are a lot more health issues that can arise from accidents or injuries.

If you experience any symptoms, your veterinarian will also check for these illnesses. When a horse is suffering every day and has little possibility of rehabilitation, many Arab owners will make the difficult decision to put it to sleep. Your Arab is unable to make this choice on his own; it is a choice of love. Sometimes, a veterinarian may tell you that you have a 10% chance of making a full recovery if you can afford to pay $5,000 for treatment and a hospital stay. A 10% possibility does not come with a lot of money for certain Arab owners. You might never have any health issues until far into your 20s if you buy an Arab who is 5-6 years old and in excellent health. It's typical to ride your horse until he's over thirty years old or older.

You might decide to cover your horse with a blanket on chilly evenings if you live somewhere where the temperature falls into the 20s and 30s. Do you think it would feel better to have your Arab wearing a coat, and does he grow a very long winter coat? In any case, an Arab will benefit from a nighttime blanket to be warm and dry.

The winter water trough for your Arab is another thing to think about. A plug-in heater that may be placed in the trough for the winter is available at many stables. The water will never freeze if you use a plug-in heater. Your Arab will probably stick his nose through the ice to get water during the night if there is no electricity. If water is available during the freeze, you can remove the ice in the morning and replenish the trough. During the colder months, controlling the ice and flowing water can prove challenging.

Activities that Stimulate the Mind

A big inflated ball that occasionally has markings similar to a football is used for play by certain horses, or they are taught how to play with one. Your Arab may play with it independently if you buy one and place it in his paddock. If he doesn't seem interested, you can incorporate it into his round pen training later on, and who knows? He might grow intrigued. In his stall, you can also hang a ball for playtime.

Arabs can be utilised for a variety of equestrian pursuits, including contests, if preferred. Arabs are frequently utilised in endurance competitions because of their reputation for endurance. The majority of races are 50 or 100 miles long. Arab and winning cyclists can finish 100 miles in 14–15 hours. That indicates a travel speed of more than seven miles per hour on average. Although horses of any breed can compete, Arabian horses typically win at the highest levels due to their innate endurance and stamina. Although Arab horses are preferred by some riders for barrel racing, Quarter Horses are more frequently used in rodeo competitions. Although other breeds are usually used in hunter/jumper contests, some riders opt to enter an Arab.

Arabs are frequently regarded as the most beautiful horse in the competition and make good show horses. Arabian horses are willing to carry you many miles in a single day and make great trail horses. Even though you have a 16-hour workday in the summer, your Arab will take you for the entire day if you so desire. Later in this book, we'll cover more about other cognitively stimulating activities.

Getting Along With Your Arab

Getting Your Arab to Get Along with Everyone: A Guide

It's crucial to socialize your Arab from an early age. Are you aware of the reason? A horse that has had proper socialization will not be hostile or afraid of people or dogs. He is aware that both people and dogs exist and do not always pose a threat to his safety. Conversely, an unsocialized horse perceives the world as a threat and responds accordingly. The presence of people or other canines frightens and threatens him. Thus, you must begin acclimating your Arab as soon as you get him home. Acclimatize him to living with dogs and other people.

Viewpoint (Yours)

Your Arab can see right through your attitude. You are like a book to him. He can tell when you are angry with him. Additionally, he is able to detect when you are upset, and he won't accept that it isn't related to him. As a result, you should always be proactive and have a positive attitude while socializing. When your Arab senses your positive energy, they will bond more easily. Be kind, loving, patient, and supportive at all times.

Express your pride and joy more than your annoyance or dissatisfaction. If you do become frustrated, take a moment to yourself, breathe deeply, and engage in a different activity with your Arab before coming back when you're both relaxed and in control. Your secret to success when training your Arab will be positivity. Refrain from pushing your Arab or losing your temper, as this can negatively impact both your training sessions and overall outcomes.

Training your Arab to become the kind of horse you want him to be when you are riding him later is a major component of socializing him. The first several months of his training form him into the Arab he becomes. As a result, you should put in the most effort and concentrate on your final objective during this time. Therefore, make sure you have a strategy, follow it, be consistent, and be clear about what you expect from him. When he follows your instructions, show your genuine happiness and excitement by rewarding him generously for his good behaviour.

You'll be astounded at how proficient you are at raising your new Arab if you adhere to these principles. Creating the unique connection you wish to have with your Arab partner for the rest of his life is a significant component of socialization. This can only be accomplished by showing him that you are the herd's leader. However, you also want to let him know that you are best friends and that you love him. Your Arab friend will become your most devoted and caring friend ever if you follow the advice in this training guide and treat him like a best friend right away. When you approach social situations, pretend that you want to be friends with this Arab, but make sure you also establish yourself as the head of the group and the dominant buddy. Maintain your firmness while remaining soft. Give instructions without being harsh or aggressive.

Aggression is never a better socialization strategy for Arabs than firmness.

When & How to Make Friends with an Arab

As early as a few hours old, your Arab starts the socialization process. He interacts with his mother and, if any other horses are available, a few other horses until then. It goes without saying that you cannot expect an Arab to pick up riding skills from his mother. From a very young age, the Arab must be exposed to and accustomed to human touch mainly because your Arab's maturity is greatly influenced by this, the most formative period of his life. When you let your Arab into your life, he is a little older. Don't stress about how well you are training him. All it will take is a little more time from you. You must begin treating your Arab like the alpha from the moment you acquire him. Talk to him, touch him, and move his body. Assimilate him to being managed by people. Each time you remove him from his stall, give him a brush. He'll discover that you're harmless, that this is fun, and that he can trust his new human herdsman. Give your Arab exposure to a variety of settings. Take him on rides outside or stroll along a path with lots of grass, plants, animals, and other people strolling, exploring, and having picnics. Take him to your neighbourhood lake, the beach, a stream, a pond, etc. Here's the main idea. Play around with it, be imaginative, and show him a variety of environments, including beaches and trails, as well as natural surroundings. He might be exposed to a slow-moving car if you have to go along a gravel road to reach a trail, depending on your situation.

Sounds like cars, trains, planes, and traffic may be familiar to your Arab. He will grow accustomed to all of the various settings and noises that he encounters. You might have to transport your Arab in a horse trailer if you are moving him to different locations. This teaches him that being curious is OK instead of being scared of a wide range of unfamiliar and unusual things. An astute Arab makes a fine horse.

Allow your friends to meet your Arab so he can become accustomed to them and discover that he can tolerate a variety of individuals. You don't want him to grow unduly dependent on you to the point that he starts to doubt other people. You will become closely bonded to your Arab if you take the time to spend bonding with them. It also teaches him how to behave with you and other people in a way that is appropriate and inappropriate. It tells him that you are a kind, dependable owner who values him and that spending time with you is joyful and enjoyable. To keep him interested and busy, it's a good idea to locate and develop a variety of mentally and physically demanding activities. Reminder: You must provide your Arab with some alone time. This helps him learn that it's OK to be nervous when you're not around to form a bond. A couple of times a day, let him graze alone in his paddock or pasture for at least an hour or two. Please do not approach him, whether he is by himself or with other horses.

To stop undesirable habits from developing in your Arab:

Don't be afraid to correct them.

Tell him "No" forcefully if he nips your arm.

When he fidgets when being touched at the hitching rail, tell him "No."

Early instruction on what is acceptable and unacceptable can help him become a more obedient horse and reduce the need for corrective action in the future.

He will learn that you are in charge and that he must pay attention to you if you stop any negative behaviour and start a positive one in its place. He really wants something from you, believe it or not. Start by telling him what actions are appropriate and what are not. Be stern but not mean.

Yelling and physical punishment should be avoided since these behaviours can cause lifelong harm to your Arab. You want him to respect you with a sense of pride in his heart, not to be terrified of you. All you need to do to redirect your Arab child's behaviour while disciplining them is to say a strong "No" and move them to another activity. It's time to begin gently teaching your Arab now. Naturally, we go into great detail about that in this book on horse training.

Additionally, show him around his stall and paddock and explain that they are secure places for him to go for solitude and weather protection. Never use the paddock as a punishment; otherwise, you risk instilling in him a deep dislike and a lifelong avoidance of it. It won't take long to discover that your Arab adores his paddock and connects it to fresh water, hay, grains, vitamins, and safety.

It is necessary to arrange for a farm visit from your reliable veterinarian to make sure your Arab is healthy and up to date on immunizations and worming. Pay attention to any advice given regarding nutrition, exercise, training, and any health issues.

When your Arab's hooves get too long, keep an eye on them and make an appointment with your reliable farrier to have them trimmed. Pay attention to every piece of advice given, such as if your Arab would benefit from wearing shoes or if they have powerful hooves. Here are some suggestions that you may decide to heed.

Attitude (Yours): You should start rigorous training as soon as your Arabian horse is comfortable in his pasture. That is to say, you can now teach him things on a long lead line or in a circular enclosure with success. We'll go into great detail about this in our next chapters. To help him become acclimated to his surroundings, make sure you stroll with him. To help him overcome his concerns and learn to accept the world as it is, expose him to a wide range of people, horses, and locations. An Arab's socialization process lasts their entire lives. You can't keep him in the paddock, never let him interact with people, and then expect him to act normally when he does. Training and socializing your Arab is a lifetime endeavour. Daily little steps will make a big difference.

Fear Embracing and Getting Over It

Remember that horses experience periods of fear imprinting. In these stages, phobias may emerge in your horse. Any unfavourable stimuli have the potential to permanently damage your horse, giving him a lifelong terror.

For example, if a guy mistreats your horse during this phase, he may develop a fear of all men. If a child is constantly tugging on his tail, he may develop a fear towards children.

Try to keep your horse from being scared by things that terrify him, such as loud noises like fireworks on July 4th, shouting in rage, or activities that could cause him unnecessary harm. At no point in his life should you be overly strict with him; instead, be kind. Take him on frequent walks around the stables to expose him to normal environmental stimuli, such as traffic and loud music, to help him overcome his scared attitude and learn that most stimuli are harmless. He will become less fearful the more you expose him to the outside world.

Naturally, some horses experience strange phobias. When he was left alone in the stables without any other horses to accompany him, my horse became fearful. Every day, I took him farther and farther. I would force him to go a little farther and stand for five minutes every day before I came back. I said to him, "Good boy, good boy, good boy," over and over each time. We had gone far enough after approximately five minutes for him to lose sight of the other horses. We carried on for an hour-long trail ride as he didn't appear to be experiencing any more concerns about it. He never again felt afraid to go out on his own. For both of us, it took an entire bag of goodies to get over that one. On the bright side, we did manage to get a good amount of exercise.

For example, your horse may develop anxiety when it crosses a tarp on the lawn. I wonder whether he was afraid he would trip, fall, or slip. For whatever reason, he refused to use the tarp as a walkway. This was resolved when he saw that another horse was led over the tarp and that the animal had not suffered any harm. His eyes showed surprise, and his ears sprang straight up. He never again felt afraid of it after that since he followed the other horse over the tarp. Make sure to repeatedly tell him, "good boy," whenever he conquers a fear. Let him understand that he won't be harmed by the things he fears. Assist him in forming constructive associations rather than destructive ones.

Your horse may develop timidity if he has a negative encounter with a person, another horse, or any other animal. However, if you take the time to help him overcome this fear and recondition him, it need not last forever.

It's a good idea to show him that not everyone is the Unabomber by exposing him to horses, other animals, and nice, joyful people. For obvious reasons, you would want to stay away from someone who has been to the stables and yelled at your Arab. Help him get over his phobia of people by exposing him to other calmer, more gentle individuals. A key component of socializing your Arab is getting over your fear.

You might also want to show him other aspects of who you are. If you're an adult male with a beard, you can shave it off and wear a hat. In addition, if you so choose (I heard it grows back thicker). Instead of pants or jeans, you can wear a dress, shorts or sunglasses.

You can even switch up your hairstyle, shampoo, and aftershave by using a different scent. He'll be aware of these modifications. He will come to accept the fact that occasionally, your appearance or aroma changes if you keep talking to him and reassure him that everything is OK when you look different. He won't be as anxious about change after that.

Continue reading to learn how to look after your new best buddy.

Naturopathic Hair Training

The impression that most people have is that in order to effectively control horses, you must have mental control over them. This is the reason why many trainers use a lead rope or harness to teach a horse how to stop and start. What options do you have, though, if you lack these supplements? Which technique can you employ to manage the hour? If you have spent a lot of time changing a tyre around a part, then you have probably asked yourself these questions.

Natural horse training is a method by which people can acquire the ability to control their horses' minds. In any situation, you will never lose control if you have control over a horse's thinking. Natural horse training is a special technique that must be carried out correctly to guarantee success.

Instead of using punishment or obedience, the training process uses calm compliance. As a trainer, self-control and discipline are essential to getting your horses to follow your lead consistently. In order to achieve this, natural horse training emphasises the establishment of a bond and a sense of security and comfort for the horse. Through this explanation, natural horse training appears simple, but it's actually a very challenging programme to learn.

Get your horse to pay attention to you before you can begin this training strategy. In order to accomplish this, you must also give your hours your undivided focus. Pay attention to what your horse is doing and avoid allowing distractions during the training session.

You and the horse must be able to concentrate and pay attention. Should you find it unable to continue doing this for extended periods, you should begin training in smaller increments and gradually increase your time. Ideally, you should begin with a minimum of ten minutes of training time.

Not only should you pay attention to your hire, but you should also take into account the input they are giving you. Do the eyes and ears convey any messages? What is the breathing pattern of the horse? Are their reactions the same as they were the previous time you worked with them? You may help the hourly pay notice to you by paying attention to these items. Look for a trigger that makes your horses do what you want them to voluntarily do, and then use this consistently.

Relaxation and rhythm are essential to natural horse training. As you go closer to the horse, your movements should be rhythmic. Relax when you approach the horse or statue. Your breathing is very important and needs to be carefully monitored. Horses are observant of your behaviour and will sense the tension in you. In the event of an unforeseen or atypical event, this relaxation and rhythm are crucial.

Once you have mastered these two basic features, you can advance in natural horse training. However, don't lose heart if everything goes perfectly the first day or week. It frequently takes many months for horses to develop a non-predatory system through natural horse training. Even while it's known as natural horse training, that doesn't guarantee everyone will experience it that way.

To genuinely manage your time, you must possess the necessary mental self-control. Here's where a lot of hard work will be required. Numerous accomplished natural horse trainers have years of experience. Therefore, don't give up if your initial attempt doesn't work. All you have to do is remember to take your time and be patient; in doing so, your horse will be patient with you. You will quickly notice the advantages that natural horse training has to offer when you do this.

Six Not the Same

If you've ever owned a fantastic horse—a unicorn—that comes only once in a lifetime, you understand how difficult it is to find another one. They are never the same, no matter how hard you try to find the same in terms of age, colour, breed, bloodline, height, shape, mental capacity, etc. Since I was eighteen, I had searched far and wide for another barrel horse that might match the small bay mare I had won on as a young girl in terms of consistency, intelligence, athleticism, and beauty.

My second horse was my unicorn. I trained a small bay mare myself. We had won our first rodeo together, in the pole bending, when I was eleven years old, and she was five. After that, we kept winning, and when I realised her career was about to expire, I started looking for a replacement.

Initially, I looked for a horse with a build similar to my small mare. It should be possible to compete at almost the same level with the same athletic ability, but that has never actually worked. She was always more willing and intelligent than they were.

I looked for someone who was the same age as her, the same colour, and who had her urge to run, but neither of those characteristics gave me what I wanted.

At last, I decided to go back to her breeder and get a horse that might be closer to her genetics.

She was a longtime friend of my dad's who served as our farrier over the majority of my adolescent years. The father reared a few children and had a few broodmares. By chance, he was still in possession of my mare's dam. By that dam, he also had a two-year-old filly up for sale. The filly was little, but my mare was too, considering her age. I got her expecting her to be another fantastic barrel horse.

In the end, the only things they had in common were size and lineage.

I gave the little filly the name Bull because I anticipated that she would have a stocky, short build like a bulldog as an adult. After a year, she showed no signs of growth. She had not gained any weight and remained little, standing at less than fourteen hands tall. Despite my best efforts, it was evident by the time she was four that she would never grow into a large horse. Her physique was slender, with very little muscle down her legs.

Bull's one redeeming quality was her extreme gentleness. She could be trained to ride anywhere in about two weeks, and breaking her in took even less time. I took her for a ride across the farms and down the road. She was so relaxed and easygoing that I rode her around with small children, something I would never do with a young horse.

Although it was difficult to give up my hope of owning another fantastic barrel horse that was bred similarly to my first, I had to accept that the best thing Bull could hope to do in life was to be a joy to ride.

The Bull was sold to a kind family who cherished her for many years. This experience taught me not to expect the same outcomes from a horse just because of ancestry.

7 Can You Identify This Horse?

You know those TV ads that entice young men and women to enlist in the military? Typically, they include a young person standing up for someone who is being bullied or in need of assistance. The soon-to-be soldier inspires you with a great sense of bravery as you watch. As they defend others and speak up for what they believe to be right, you can see the passion in their eyes. That's how I feel about horses on occasion.

Throughout my life, I have frequently come across horses in need of assistance. I went to look at a large grey horse in North Texas as an example. I thought he might make a good barrel horse, and the advertisement said little girls were racing him on play days. I decided to take a chance and take a look at this nine-year-old, really well-bred grey horse since the price was approximately $1,500.

As I got closer to the horse, I saw a large red patch on his stunning white coat. It was right there on his neck, exactly where you would shoot it. Initially, I assumed he had recently had an injection to enable him to walk without exhibiting lameness. The horse's unsteady gait made the shot ineffective. Aside from that, the horse was incredibly skinny and malnourished. I said nothing because the man displaying the horse to me was accompanied by his two small daughters. Not only did I not ride the horse, but I offered to buy the gelding for $500 since I felt awful for him. Without even thinking twice, the man said yes. All I wanted was to keep this horse alive. Whatever life I could give the miserable animal would be better than what he had if that man was ready to medicate the horse and lie to me instead of trying to heal him. I urgently needed a barrel horse prospect and didn't have much money, but I couldn't turn down this opportunity to help. I was willing to go to any lengths, even at my own expense, to help the gelding since he needed me.

I was moved to assist another horse a few years later. My acquaintance had bought a small bay stud colt from the neighbourhood auction barn. It was a two-year-old with a mane and tail that looked scruffy. He had become so pale that he resembled a sorrel rather than a bay. My pal had him crippled when I first saw him. He managed to put the saddle on somehow, but he had come to the conclusion that the best way to break him was to just keep him hobbled and saddled until he stopped fighting. I asked my buddy if she would be interested in selling him while I observed the animal, trying to make sense of what was happening.

Now, I grew up breaking colts the traditional manner. I learned from my dad to "sack them out" before attempting to ride them until they stopped bucking. I got the chance to experiment with this strict approach when I was a teenager. I discovered that it was rather challenging. As soon as I tied a young horse to the fence and began rising in the saddle, the link I had formed with them throughout the cool-down and acclimatisation phase was broken. And I always found it much more difficult and uncomfortable to buck them than it was for them. I first encountered the round pen approach in college. I was certain that this was the proper approach after learning how it operated and witnessing the incredible outcomes it generated. In addition to being easier on both the horse and the rider, it preserved the relationship that had grown between them. I became intolerant of the "old school" approaches to colt breaking after discovering this new technique.

My friend accepted my $500 offer for the colt when I called him the following day.

This was the start of my tale of the ugly duckling. The tiny, young horse was unsightly. His conformation was not fluid at all. His front end didn't even appear to match his rear end. He had little to no muscle mass and a sharp, sloping shoulder. He was so short (I am about five feet tall) that I could see over him at approximately fourteen hands. Plus, he was a stud, and I don't want to work with studs. They intimidate me. There are plenty of gentlemanly studs out there, but I'm not interested in working with one myself. Though his pedigree was not particularly spectacular, at least he had pedigree papers.

I had to get Ace first, as I had decided to call him. I was glad to give him the love and care he so desperately needed. Every day, I would groom him. Being a professional show horse trainer, my father-in-law would frequently drop by to check on the horses that my spouse and I were training. He was not delighted with the new colt. He was unable to comprehend my purchase of him. All he could do was shake his head at what he saw as a bad investment.

We proved it to him, though!

Following three months of nurturing, Ace started to swell...and swell...and swell! He developed nearly a full hand! That demonstrated the power of proper diet and care in enabling a young horse to realise his full potential. He grew to be about sixteen hands tall in just a year!

The skinny little stud colt grew broader and longer in addition to taller! Now, his tail and mane were thick and shiny. His conformation became more uniform, and his coat went dark bay. He was a stunning swan now. My father-in-law was astounded by what he observed with his own eyes.

How could you have known he would grow into such a gorgeous, large gelding? He enquired.

All I could say was that something inside me told me he was more than what we initially saw. He merely needed assistance to realise his potential.

I routinely worked with the colt. He grew accustomed to being ridden and saddled. To put a handle on Ace and get him started on cattle, I sent him to a young man. He began training him to be a team roping horse and would track steers on him while swinging a rope. Ace had gained some experience and was well on his way to starting his first job when I got him back.

Ace was riding really nicely now, so I worked him on the barrels. He adjusted to them fairly nicely. He was fit and open to trying anything I asked. He was only four years old, yet he possessed the cerebral and physical maturity of a ten-year-old. He was an old man caught in the body of a young horse, I would joke. Before long, he was regularly following the pattern.

I opted to sell my horses at this point in my life because I was having financial problems. I calculated that if they sold for a decent price, I would still have enough money to buy another cheap potential.

The Ace was put up for sale.

I priced him at four times the costs I had invested in him. For a horse that I had not even owned for the previous two years, it would be a very nice profit.

In a month, he sold.

A really kind man arrived and gave Ace a try. He intended to utilise him as his wife's barrel horse and as his roping horse. Even though I knew he would have a wonderful home, I couldn't help but cry when I accepted the sale. My heart ached. It was one of the most difficult choices I had ever had to make. I have shed tears over very few of the horses that I have owned and trained, but they are all very dear to me. Ace was among those people. I sobbed myself to sleep that night. Although monetarily and for the horse, it was the right choice, it was still difficult.

It was almost six years later.

I occasionally wondered how Ace was doing and gave him some thought. By then, I realised he was most likely a finished team roping horse and possibly running barrel races. It proved that I was correct.

I once travelled to Waco, Texas, to witness my closest friend compete in a team roping competition. We met in college and immediately clicked since we both loved horses and dogs. I couldn't wait to go support her because she was a strong header.

I went looking for her behind the arena when she completed roping. I was squeezing past horses and riders as I made my way down the lengthy hallways connecting the warm-up sections when I noticed a familiar face. It was an elderly man I had known since I was a child. I had competed with him on a ranch rodeo team when I was a child, and he was an avid team roper. He spotted me as he looked down.

Hello, Jana! He uttered those words. And he immediately moved on to a question that really took me off guard after a few minutes of formalities. Can you identify this horse?"

Not at all. No, I don't.

"He was your property. About a year ago, I got him to rope on.

Actually. What is his name?"

"Ace."

You could have easily taken me out with a feather, though. The horse I had adored was standing there, and he was gorgeous! This man was the one to whom I had sold him. I felt very happy that Ace was leading a happy life.

Exams by a Vet for Your Friesian Horse

Before committing to a new horse, I will always get it checked out by a veterinarian. I usually won't get another checkup for another one to four years or until I start to notice any health issues. I want the veterinarian to weigh and examine his eyes, teeth, and hooves every time they visit. To maintain your Friesian horse healthy for the duration of its life, additional general care requirements must be met in addition to adequate nutrition and exercise.

These consist of regular veterinarian care for teeth, feet, and immunisations; regular grooming and weatherproofing; and management of parasites. A reputable veterinarian will recommend foods and drugs for treatment. Elderly horses (those over 20 years of age) should see their veterinarian at least twice a year, if not more regularly, as sickness is more common and easier to diagnose in older animals.

Your veterinarian could suggest regular blood tests as part of a wellness programme for your Friesian horse. I have owned my horses for ten years, and they are all over twenty years old. My closest friends treat my stables more like a retirement community! Right now, only one of the three can be ridden, but I want to give them the best possible life. These horses, who reside in a small portion of paradise, are fortunate and content.

Issues with Your Friesian Horse's Health

Although numerous things can happen even before the age of 20, the majority of health issues will manifest beyond that age. The majority of Friesian horses experience accidents or injuries before they experience health issues. It is usual for Friesian horses to have two conditions:

digestive system
defence mechanism
Additional Horse Conditions:
tetanus
Cushing's
Constriction (Distemper)
Influenza
Pneumonia in the nose
Encephalomyelitis in Horses
rabies
Worms in the stomach
Colic

Laminitis

Sadly, there are a lot more health issues that can arise from accidents or injuries.

If you experience any symptoms, your veterinarian will also check for these illnesses. When a Friesian horse is suffering on a daily basis and has little possibility of rehabilitation, many owners will have to make the difficult decision to put their horse to sleep. Your Friesian Horse is incapable of making this choice on his own; it is a choice of love. Sometimes, a veterinarian will tell you that you have a 10% chance of making a full recovery if you can afford to pay $5,000 or more for treatment and a hospital stay.

Some owners of Friesian horses don't have much money to throw away on a 10% chance. You might not have any health issues until well into your horse's 20s if you get a 5–6-year-old Friesian who is in excellent health. It's typical to ride your Friesian horse until he's over thirty years old or older.

You might want to cover your Friesian horse with a blanket on chilly evenings if you live somewhere where the temperature falls between twenty and thirty degrees. Do you think it would feel better to have your Friesian horse wearing a coat, and does he grow a really long winter coat? In any case, an overnight blanket will help keep your Friesian horse dry and toasty.

The winter water trough for your Friesian horse is another thing to think about. A plug-in heater that may be placed in the trough for the winter is available at many stables. The water will never freeze if you use a plug-in heater. Your Friesian horse will probably pierce the ice with his nose to get to water throughout the night if there is no electricity. If water is available during the freeze, you can remove the ice in the morning and replenish the trough. During the colder months, controlling the ice and flowing water can prove challenging.

Activities that Stimulate the Mind

A big inflated ball that is occasionally marked to resemble a football is something that some Friesian horses will play with or be taught to play with. Your Friesian horse might play with it by himself if you buy one and place it in his pasture. If he doesn't seem interested, you can incorporate it into his round pen training later on, and who knows? He might grow intrigued. In his stall, you can also hang a ball for playtime.

Friesian horses are useful for a variety of tasks, including competitions, if required. Certain horses are frequently employed in racing contests because of their reputation for having high long-distance speed. Although quarter horses are more frequently used in rodeo events, some riders choose to use other horses for barrel racing. Although different breeds are usually used in hunter/jumper competitions, some riders select Thoroughbreds for these events.

Arabian horses are frequently regarded as the most beautiful animals in the event and make superb show horses. Numerous Friesian horses are willing to go long distances in a single day and make fantastic trail horses. If you want, you can spend the entire day with your Friesian horse. Later in this book, we'll cover more about other cognitively stimulating activities.

Review: Horseback Riding

Are you a fan of horses? Do you prefer to ride them over machinery? Then you should definitely read this book. This book will assist you in caring for horses and teach you riding techniques. The history of horseback riding extends back to the earliest stages of human civilization, demonstrating the age of the sport. The artwork from the earliest civilizations provides evidence of it. These illustrations suggest that the horses' primary function during battles was to haul large loads. Furthermore, historians contend that the Brahmin caste of India was the first group of people to ride horses, whereas Chinese equestrians were the first to produce horses.

We may still observe the influence of earlier civilizations when we look at modern equestrian riding styles. History demonstrates that every civilization had a unique method for mounting horses, and numerous new forms were developed based on existing approaches.

English and Western horseback riding are the most well-known riding disciplines. Westerners mostly employ these two approaches for two distinct goals. Although the instruments and goals of the two styles differed, the techniques employed in both were essentially the same. Cowboys mostly employ western horseback riding to carry out their daily chores. In contrast, the English approach is primarily employed in racing or disciplinary situations.

Although both forms of horseback riding are equally well-known among riders, they are utilized interchangeably due to their respective functions. The tools being utilized differ in addition to their differing uses. The purpose of the saddle in Western horseback riding is to give the rider perfect balance so they may carry out their duties with ease and confidence. Furthermore, because they are designed for prolonged usage, Western saddles weigh far more than English saddles.

Knowing the various riding styles is just the first step; the next critical step is to comprehend riding tactics. The first important thing to remember when riding a horse is to maintain proper posture. The correct posture will be identified by riding style, but it is still necessary for the rider to learn how to sit straight, with their head and shoulders up. In addition to keeping the rider from falling off, this stance promotes comfort while riding. Understanding the sort of Horse comes next, followed by posture. Horses differ in temperament, stature, and breed. A trained horse with a composed demeanour is the ideal choice for a novice horseback rider.

In addition to knowing the Horse's personality and breed, the rider needs to take better care of him to ensure a safe and pleasurable ride. Taking care of a horse is not a difficult chore. Before and after riding, there are a few things to remember, such as examining the hooves, removing the saddle, caressing the head, and releasing the girth. The

Horse will remain in top riding condition if you follow these easy care instructions.

Prior to embarking on a horseback riding experience, it is imperative to consider the appropriate attire for the rider. Because of the differences in saddle forms, riders in both designs must wear different clothing. At the same time, western horseback riding allows riders to dress casually, such as in jeans; English equestrian riding requires riders to wear breeches because they offer more comfort and safety. Additionally, the rider's shoes should be chosen carefully since they could become lodged in the stirrup and cause an accident. To avoid any potential mishaps, riders are typically instructed to wear shoes with tiny heels and hard soles.

These are the things that must be completed before beginning a horseback ride; the important skills for mounting a horse are crucial since they guarantee a safer ride. The first and most crucial step is to approach the Horse properly. The

Horse will be able to see and interact with the rider if the rider approaches the animal from the side, according to expert advice. In order to prevent overtaxing the Horse, the rider should, secondly, mount and gently settle into the saddle.

Anyone can enjoy the exhilarating experience of horseback riding with the aid of all this advice and knowledge. For enjoyment and perfection, people must still practise a lot. Research on horseback riding has demonstrated that once learned, it can assist in the treatment of a variety of physical and mental problems in people. Thus, begin training and tending to your equine immediately and relish the revitalizing sensation of equestrian riding.

It's mutually soothing, I can guarantee you, before the long day starts.

One of the most healing and uplifting experiences you will have with your Horse is this one. As much as you enjoy brushing him, he will adore being brushed. While you are brushing him, converse with him. Talk to him frequently using his name. Say "good boy" each time he stands up straight. Give the order, "Stand," if he starts to try to move away from you or around. Once he stops moving, praise him by saying, "Good Boy," and telling him to stop repeatedly. When they are young, some horses may try to bite or kick you. NEVER ALLOW EITHER TO OCCUR! You must take precautions for your safety whenever you are around your Horse. Make sure he's not about to kick you by keeping a close eye on him. He might be considering it if he is standing with one leg bent back. If you never let him, he will never bite or kick you.

To ensure that he misses his kick if he attempts, you might want to give him some room while you move around him. You have to smack his nose away and tell him, "No biting," if he attempts to chew on your arm. You only need to backhand lightly. If you hit your Horse hard, never hit it again. He will never consider biting or kicking you until he has fully bonded with you. If necessary, brush his entire body, neck, face, and legs. You'll clean every inch of his body, starting with the muck and working your way down to the dust.

Always keep oneself safe. Use a detangling brush to gently remove any tangles from his forelock and mane. Some tangles require cutting out because they are so severe. Once the mane is finished, do the same with his tail. Maybe you can stand right behind him and brush his tail in the future.

We advise you to start by standing to one side of his back and softly brushing his tail to one side. Keep in mind that you and your Horse may bond quickly or slowly. It is ideal for everyone when selecting a horse if he seems devoted to you PRIOR to purchase. That will guarantee that the bonding process happens considerably faster. The bonding process includes everything you do in the beginning with your Horse. You are building a lasting, healthy, and pleasant relationship with your Horse, little by little. Please savour every moment while you go.

Taking a bath

You might feel the need to give your new best friend lots of baths. But remember, his skin and hair are kept healthy by his natural oils. Washing too much can remove those oils. As a result, it is advisable to bathe your Horse just once during the warm months of the year. Ensure that you purchase a warm-water washing stall and high-quality horse shampoo, such as Mane & Tail Shampoo.

1. Walk your Horse into the laundry room.

2. Attach your Horse's lead rope to the hitching rail with care now.

3. You can turn on the water once your Horse is inside the washing stall. Use your fingers to feel the water's temperature before soaking your Horse. Make sure the water is lukewarm and pleasant.

4. Wet your Horse's entire body before massaging it with the shampoo to produce a light foam. Take care not to use so little that you can't get a rich lather or so much that you can't rinse it

all out. Do your best to stay out of his mouth and eyes. Rinse face when bathing if needed.

5. Tip: Give his head a final bath. This is the bit he would find objectionable.

6. Now rinse him thoroughly using lukewarm water.

Gently work the shampoo out with your hands from top to bottom. Do this several times to get all the shampoo out so his natural oils can get busy keeping him healthy.

7. Now turn the water off and dry him some with a towel. Rub him down thoroughly. Lead him to a dry spot in the sun to let him dry. Keep in mind, at his first chance, he will roll in the dirt or the mud directly after he is washed. It is better if he is completely dry before you let that happen.

Hooves

Your Horse needs his hooves to grip while walking and running. You should clean your Horse's hooves every time you take him out of the stall. You would have learned in your lessons how to use a hoof pick to scrape out the mud, manure, and other debris stuck in the hooves. It is important as small pieces of gravel can get stuck and cause injury to your Horse. Pick up each foot individually and clean each hoof.

What is Horse Training?

Before we get into why horses are trained, it is important to have a clear understanding of exactly what horse training is. Horse training refers to the repetitive execution of various exercises in a bid to develop some familiarity with the same from a physical and mental point of view. Any horse training exercises are specifically meant to help the Horse develop some type of fitness and sharpness. As a horse trainer or owner, it is vital to have an understanding of the difference between mental and physical horse training. This will help you in understanding why horse training exercises tend to be numerous and varied.

Horse Training Objectives

As stated above, horse training is not done haphazardly and must be aimed at achieving certain objectives. Basically, horse training can be aimed at making the Horse develop various habits. This mainly refers to all training efforts meant to make the Horse develop their mental understanding of certain gestures and signals. This can include training the Horse to understand how and when the owner or trainer wants it to come off or onto a trailer. It can also train the Horse to stand still as a saddle is put in place and the rider mounts it.

On the other hand, horse training can be used to enhance the physical fitness of the Horse. These exercises are aimed at developing a horse's muscle system in a bid to make it stronger and more capable, depending on the intended application of the Horse. Such exercises will be aimed at making the Horse run faster, enhance its endurance, and even jump higher. These tend to be the most popular horse training exercises and the first to come to mind when people hear about horse training.

Reasons for Horse Training

Another important aspect of learning how to train a horse involves understanding exactly why horses require training. Why do horse owners invest a lot of time and money in making sure that their horses are trained every day? Answering this question sufficiently will go a long way in helping you appreciate the need for horse training in the first place and why perfect execution is essential in enhancing your Horse's quality of life.

Preparing them to be Easy to Ride

Most people who own horses today normally use them for riding. This riding can be for leisure purposes or high-performance racing. It is important to note that even though horses have been domesticated for centuries, the fact that they come with varying temperaments means that they must be trained over and over again so as to be able to tolerate human contact and, subsequently, riding. It is important to note that riding does not just cover the ability to saddle and mount a horse but also the knowledge that is involved. The Horse needs to understand the commands of the rider and hence make riding possible and safe.

Enhance Performance

Horse training involves conducting a host of exercises meant to tone the Horse and enhance its performance. Horses are used for racing and jumping as well; to enhance their performance in these applications, it is necessary to make sure that they are in great physical condition. The necessary muscles must be strong and sturdy enough. There is a host of different horse training activities and exercises meant to increase the fitness of a horse. During regular training sessions, it is important to know the collection of exercises meant to improve the physical performance of the Horse in its field of operation.

Cooling down after your training session

Riding-Out (Hacking-Out)

Once your young Horse is sufficiently obedient to the basic aids, he should be regularly taken on short rides in the company of another steady horse. This will give him more courage, and he will learn to enjoy being ridden out.

When you ride in your schooling arena, the surroundings are more or less the same every day, and it is relatively easy to gain your Horse's attention and keep him "on the job". When you ride out, the scenery is constantly changing, and horses like to enjoy the view as much as anyone. In fact, the changing view is of more importance to your Horse than it is to you. As a creature of 'flight' rather than 'fight', it is essential for a horse to spot danger from a distance and to know which way he may be able to escape. On the other hand, when you are riding, you want your Horse to accept you as his leader, to trust you and to keep his attention on you.

The younger and more novice your Horse is, the more important it is to let him stop if he wants to, look closely at "potential new dangers," and look around generally to take in his surroundings. As the partnership with your Horse develops, he will become more willing to accept your judgement, quicker to accept new experiences, and less mesmerized by everything new close by and on the distant horizon. Try to find a happy medium when hacking; do not give in to every whim, and when you decide it's time to move on, then that is what you do. However, at other times, you will want to give your Horse a chance to relax and enjoy the countryside; let him stand and absorb the view while having a little rest.

For your young Horse, the countryside can be full of dangers, from loose barking dogs to big, noisy trucks and tractors, from clothing flapping on nearby washing lines to the pigeon that flies out of the hedge just under your Horse's nose. A lot of accidents riding out result from inattention and lack of preparation on the part of the rider. A horse on a loose rein is not really under a rider's control, and if you are just sitting on your Horse like a passenger, daydreaming about your dinner or something, instead of riding him, you will be that much slower to react in the event of trouble.

Hacking out with a steady horse will keep the young Horse interested in his work and improve his confidence.

It makes sense to go out at the end of a training session in the schooling area instead of heading out with a fresh horse straight out of the stable. The first few times, just walk and trot, ideally in the company of one or two sensible, experienced horses. Let the experienced horse lead during the hack. Do not ride out in the company of a horse that shies or is bad in traffic, as your young Horse may copy him. After a few rides out, get your Horse used to being ridden level with the other Horse, and then go in front. If you meet something that frightens your Horse, he can then again be given a lead by the experienced Horse.

If you have to introduce your Horse to hack out without the company of another schoolmaster horse, ask someone to go with you on foot to help you if your Horse is frightened of passing something and choose a safe route. Do not ride your young Horse out in traffic until you have introduced him to moving cars, farm machinery, etc.

When you meet other horses for the first time when riding out alone, your Horse may either ignore them or get very excited. There is no way to predict this before it happens. If the other horses are walking along quietly, your Horse is more likely to remain calm. Therefore, one should not trot or canter closely past another horse going in the opposite direction. Always walk when you see another rider approaching you in case either of you has a problem. If your Horse does start to misbehave and buck, a neck-strap or a handful of mane will help you to stay on your Horse, which is always better than letting him realize that he can get you off, which he may then try again on another occasion.

The first canter out on a hack is easiest and most safely done going uphill. The first canter should be short, at the end of the hack and take place in familiar surroundings. Follow an experienced horse up a slight hill in a steady rising trot, allowing a 4 to 6 horse-length gap between you and the lead Horse. Let the Horse in front of you strike into a slow canter, and then ask your Horse to canter, too. Sit quietly with your seat just out of the saddle and try to keep your Horse in a steady, even canter rhythm. Gently check the rhythm of each stride with your hands to ensure an even canter stride length. If you allow the strides to get longer and longer, there may be the risk of your Horse getting out of control. When cantering uphill, a horse is less likely to increase pace and get on his forehand. When cantering down a slight slope or even on the flat, a young horse may easily get on his forehand, get unbalanced and find it more difficult to stop himself again.

Never ask for canter until your Horse is trotting calmly and in an even rhythm. A wide-open expanse in front of your Horse may only get him excited. You will have to practice cantering side by side and cantering away from other horses until your Horse does it quietly and willingly. Do not always ask for canter at the same place when out on a hack. Within no time, your Horse will canter off without having been asked to do so. Even worse, you may not be able to stop him from cantering at that spot. Instead, do your favourite canter stretches, often in trot or walk.

Chapter 4

You should brush your Gypsy Vanner Horse's coat at least four times a week and clean his hooves each time. Daily brushing is ideal when a Gypsy Vanner Horse is shedding in the Spring. He will need to shed his entire winter coat before the warm summer comes.

It's mutually soothing, I can guarantee you, before the long day starts.

This is one of the most therapeutic and bonding experiences you will have with your Gypsy Vanner Horse. As much as you enjoy brushing him, he will adore being brushed. While you are brushing him, converse with him. Talk to him frequently using his name. Say "good boy" each time he stands up straight. Give the order, "Stand," if he starts to try to move away from you or around. Once he stops moving, praise him by saying, "Good Boy," and telling him to stop repeatedly. Some Gypsy Vanner Horses may try to kick or bite you when they are new. NEVER ALLOW EITHER TO OCCUR! It is your responsibility to keep yourself safe every time you are around your Gypsy Vanner Horse. Make sure he's not about to kick you by keeping a close eye on him. He might be considering it if he is standing with one leg bent back. If you never let him, he will never bite or kick you.

To ensure that he misses his kick if he attempts, you might want to give him some room while you move around him. You have to smack his nose away and tell him, "No biting," if he attempts to chew on your arm. You only need to backhand lightly. Never hit your Gypsy Vanner Horse very hard if you do. He will never consider biting or kicking you until he has fully bonded with you. If necessary, brush his entire body, neck, face, and legs. You'll clean every inch of his body, starting with the muck and working your way down to the dust.

Always keep oneself safe. Use a detangling brush to gently remove any tangles from his forelock and mane. Some tangles require cutting out because they are so severe. Once the mane is finished, do the same with his tail. Maybe you can stand right behind him and brush his tail in the future.

We advise you to start by standing to one side of his back and softly brushing his tail to one side. Remember that bonding with your Gypsy Vanner Horse can happen quickly or slowly. When choosing your Gypsy Vanner Horse, it works best for all if he seems affectionate to you BEFORE you buy him. That will guarantee that the bonding process happens considerably faster. EVERYTHING that you do with your Gypsy Vanner Horse at the beginning is part of the bonding process. You are gradually creating a positive, healthy and life-long relationship with your Gypsy Vanner Horse. Please savour every moment while you go.

Taking a bath

You might feel the need to give your new best friend lots of baths. But remember, his skin and hair are kept healthy by his natural oils. Washing too much can remove those oils. Therefore, it is best to bathe your Gypsy Vanner Horse only once a season when it is warm outside. Make sure to buy a quality horse shampoo such as Mane & Tail Shampoo and use a washing stall with warm water. Conditioner of the same brand is available for his mane and tail.

1. Lead your Gypsy Vanner Horse into the washing stall.

2. Now gently tie your Gypsy Vanner Horse's Lead Rope to the hitching rail.

3. Once your Gypsy Vanner Horse is in the washing stall, you can start running the water. Before soaking your Gypsy Vanner Horse, test the water temperature carefully with your fingers. Make sure the water is lukewarm and pleasant.

4. Get your Gypsy Vanner Horse's entire body wet and begin rubbing in the shampoo to create a gentle lather. Take care not to use so little that you can't get a rich lather or so much that you can't rinse it all out. Do your best to stay out of his mouth and eyes. Rinse face when bathing if needed.

5. Tip: Give his head a final bath. This is the bit he would find objectionable.

6. Now rinse him thoroughly using lukewarm water.

Gently work the shampoo out with your hands from top to bottom. Do this several times to get all the shampoo out so his natural oils can get busy keeping him healthy.

7. Now turn the water off and dry him some with a towel. Rub him down

thoroughly. Lead him to a dry spot in the sun to let him dry. Keep in mind, at his first chance, he will roll in the dirt or the mud directly after he is washed. It is better if he is completely dry before you let that happen.

Hooves

Your Gypsy Vanner Horse needs his hooves to grip while walking and running. You should clean your Gypsy Vanner Horse's hooves every time that you take him out of the stall. You would have learned in your lessons how to use a hoof pick to scrape out the mud, manure, and other debris stuck in the hooves. It is important as small pieces of gravel can get stuck and cause injury to your Gypsy Vanner Horse. Pick up each foot individually and clean each hoof.

Most Gypsy Vanner Horses need to have their hooves trimmed approximately every 6-8 weeks. You can learn to do this with a trimmer and a file, or you can hire a Farrier to come and trim for you. The trimmer looks like a cross between giant pliers and a nail clipper. The file is a very large, rough file. After trimming ¼ to ½ inch, most times, the hoof can be filed smoothly with just a few strokes. Do not try to trim too short, or the hoof will begin to bleed. Some owners decide to have shoes on their Gypsy Vanner Horse every time after trimming.

Making Your Thoroughbred Horse Social

Bringing Your Thoroughbred Horse Up to Be Nice to Everyone

It's crucial to socialize your Thoroughbred horse from an early age. Are you aware of the reason? A horse that has had proper socialization will not be hostile or afraid of people or dogs. He is aware that both people and dogs exist and do not always pose a threat to his safety. Conversely, an unsocialized horse perceives the world as a threat and responds accordingly. The presence of people or other canines frightens and threatens him. Thus, you must begin socializing your Thoroughbred Horse as soon as you bring him home. Acclimatize him to living with dogs and other people.

Viewpoint (Yours)

Your thoroughbred horse can tell exactly how you feel. You are like a book to him. He can tell when you are angry with him. Additionally, he is able to detect when you are upset, and he won't accept that it isn't related to him. As a result, you should always be proactive and have a positive attitude while socializing. When he senses your positive energy, your thoroughbred horse will bond with you more deeply. Be kind, loving, patient, and supportive at all times.

Express your pride and joy more than your annoyance or dissatisfaction. If you find yourself becoming frustrated, take a moment to move away, breathe deeply, and engage your Thoroughbred Horse in a new activity. When you're feeling composed, go back. When it comes to training your Thoroughbred horse, positivity will be your key to success. Avoid being enraged or persistently pushing your thoroughbred horse, as this will negatively impact both your training experiences and overall outcomes.

Conditioning your Thoroughbred horse to become the kind of horse you want him to be when you are riding him later on is a major component of socializing him. The first several months of his training transform him into the

Thoroughbred Horse he eventually becomes. As a result, you should put in the most effort and concentrate on your final objective during this time. Therefore, make sure you have a strategy, follow it, be consistent, and be clear about what you expect from him. When he follows your instructions, show your genuine happiness and excitement by rewarding him generously for his good behaviour.

You'll be astounded at how adept you are at teaching your new Thoroughbred horse if you adhere to these principles. Developing the unique relationship you wish to have with your Thoroughbred Horse for the duration of his life is another important aspect of socializing. This can only be accomplished by showing him that you are the herd's leader. However, you also want to let him know that you are best friends and that you love him. Your Thoroughbred Horse will become the most devoted and caring companion you have ever had if you follow the proper training methods described in this manual and treat him like a best friend right away. When you approach social situations, pretend that you are interested in becoming friends with this Thoroughbred Horse, but don't forget to assert your authority as the head of the group and the dominating buddy. Maintain your firmness while remaining soft. Give instructions without being harsh or aggressive. Aggression is never a better socialization strategy for a Thoroughbred horse than firmness.

When & How to Introduce Your Horse to Others

Even only a few hours old, your thoroughbred horse has already started the socialization process. He interacts with his mother and, if any other horses are available, a few other horses until then. Naturally, a Thoroughbred horse's mother cannot teach him how to be an excellent riding horse. From a very young age, the Thoroughbred Horse needs to be exposed to and acclimated to human touch. Mainly because your Thoroughbred horse's development is greatly influenced by this period of his life, which is also the most impressionable. When you welcome your Thoroughbred Horse into your life, he is a little older. Don't worry about how well you trained him. All it will take is a little more time from you. You must begin treating your Thoroughbred Horse as the alpha from the moment you acquire him. Talk to him, touch him, and move his body. Assimilate him to being managed by people. Each time you remove him from his stall, give him a brush. He'll discover that you're harmless, that this is fun, and that he can trust his new human herdsman. Give your Thoroughbred horse a variety of environmental experiences. Take him on rides outside or stroll along a path with lots of grass, plants, animals, and other people strolling, exploring, and having picnics. Take him to your neighbourhood lake, the beach, a stream, a pond, etc. Here's the main idea. Play around with it, be imaginative, and show him a variety of environments, including beaches and trails, as well as natural surroundings. He might be exposed to a slow-moving car if you have to go along a gravel road to reach a trail, depending on your situation.

Your Thoroughbred Horse may be exposed to noises such as traffic, aeroplanes, trains, and cars. He will grow accustomed to all of the various settings and noises that he encounters. It can be necessary to transport your Thoroughbred horse in a horse trailer if you are moving him to different locations. This teaches him that being curious is okay instead of being scared of a wide range of unfamiliar and unusual things. An excellent horse is a global thoroughbred.

Allow your pals to get to know your Thoroughbred Horse so he can learn to tolerate new people and develop a diverse social circle. You don't want him to grow unduly dependent on you to the point that he starts to doubt other people. You and your Thoroughbred Horse will get quite close if you take the time to bond with them. It also teaches him how to behave with you and other people in a way that is appropriate and inappropriate. It tells him that you are a kind, dependable owner who values him and that spending time with you is joyful and enjoyable. To keep him interested and busy, it's a good idea to locate and develop a variety of mentally and physically demanding activities. Note: It's essential to provide some alone time for your thoroughbred horse. This helps him learn that it's okay to be nervous when you're not around to form a bond. A couple of times a day, let him graze alone in his paddock or pasture for at least an hour or two. Please do not approach him, whether he is by himself or with other horses.

Taking Good Care of Your Spanish Equines

Crucial Attention for Your Brand-New Andalusian Horse

It's far easier to prevent future health issues with your Andalusian horse if you start learning how to take care of him before you bring him home. Every stage of your Andalusian horse's life requires correct Nutrition, care, and exercise. Before bringing him home, you should have a veterinarian checkup. Oh, and be advised that on your first visit, it's likely he will resist or show signs of dread. He will rapidly become friendly with the veterinarian and build trust before further visits. Throughout his life, keeping him engaged both cognitively and physically will reduce problem behaviours.

Feeding Nutrition for horses is crucial to the health of your Andalusian horse. His age, degree of exercise, and breed will all influence his dietary requirements. Make sure you choose the right meal for his health. Here are some tips for choosing the right kinds of food to feed your Andalusian horse.

Dehydrated Animal Feed

Be sure to prioritize past feedings by the previous owner when selecting dry food. Alfalfa is preferred over grass hay by many horse owners. Legumes like lucerne are higher in protein than grass hay. If Andalusian horses consume so much protein, some of them become "jacked up." If your Andalusian horse seems more spirited or displays behavioural issues, pay close attention. Try grass hay, like Timothy Hay or Orchard Grass, for a week if you observe this behaviour and see if it stops. You should convert your Andalusian horse to a grass hay diet if you notice that it becomes hyperactive when fed lucerne.

Extra Vitamins, Grain or Feed

Pick a horse food that has a wide variety of vitamins and minerals in it. Supplements have been developed especially for all types of horses, including young, elderly, fat, and athletic horses. Super Supplement LMF - G is a vitamin supplement feed that I prefer to use. G is an acronym for grass hay. If you are giving lucerne to your Andalusian horse, there is another variation available. A quarter of a pound of LMF-G is fed to my horses every morning and evening. Additionally, they are given one pound of COB twice a day, which is a blend of maize, oats and barley. Due to recent weight loss, my eldest senior horse is fed an additional ½ pound of rice bran twice a day to assist her in putting on weight.

Following their morning meal, the horses are released into the pasture during the dry seasons. For the most of the day, they can graze on the grass. They can eat almost a pound of grass in a single hour. Make sure every horse has extra hay overnight if they are allowed to graze for ten hours. The majority of Andalusian horses weigh about 1000 pounds, with their shoulders and highest points measuring 15 hands. This big horse needs 20 pounds of hay per day in addition to pasture. Give your horse an extra 10 pounds of hay in the evening for the night on days when it's believed that he grazed 10 pounds of grass.

For weather-related reasons, you may choose some days to keep your Andalusian horse inside the paddock. You will need to provide each horse with about 20 pounds of hay in their stall on those days. The grass has a very high sugar content in the early spring. The majority of horses should only spend a brief period in the pasture in the spring when new growth is expected. There is a second new growth season in the autumn in some years and locations. Because every region of the nation is unique, pay attention to where you live.

This restriction on lush, quick-growing grass is because of the possibility of overindulging in sugar content and "founder" in your Andalusian horse. A foundering Andalusian horse is susceptible to laminitis. Laminitis has the potential to kill and severely impair your Andalusian horse. Limiting pasture time at these times of fresh grass growth is a safer way to prevent disease.

Wet Cuisine

An elderly and toothless Andalusian horse may benefit from a diet high in moist horse food. If a horse is unable to chew its hay, it can be replaced with soaked hay pellets. To prolong the life of your Andalusian horse, feed it the soaked pellets even if it hasn't had teeth in years. Typically, your Andalusian horse may begin to lose teeth at the age of 25. They might not need to transition to a wet food diet for at least five years.

Diet of Fresh Foods

Your Andalusian horse may benefit greatly from a fresh food diet because it more nearly resembles what he would consume on his own in the wild. However, if he is fed only grass, you have to be careful not to let him get fired. A lot of horses can survive without extra hay, food, or vitamins. Plenty of horses can live in pasture year-round without ever getting laminitis. Your Andalusian horse must have a place to go to in order to escape the heat or bad weather if they are pastured. Your Andalusian horse needs constant access to FRESH and clean water if it is a grazing horse. We would advise installing an automated irrigation system.

Practice More.

The preceding variables all have an impact on the horse's glide.

It's crucial to know that practically all horses can walk on level ground. Not every horse has the fifteen or twenty feet of sliding talent. The horse must be able to halt and slide as well as have the desire to do so in order to accomplish this.

The outcome of your training session will be unpleasant and severe for both of you if you try to teach a horse that is not inclined to perform extended sliding stops. Even while your horse will eventually become fearful of you, it won't consistently stop. Thus, it's critical to confirm that your horse desires to be a long, slippery stopper.

In what way, then, can you discern his desire to learn? You stand a fair chance of teaching him to halt a long slide if he can stop at a trot or slow slope with ease. This is presuming your horse has sufficient energy to maintain the hard stop and that you have gradually pushed the stop.

However, it's not worth attempting to teach your horse to stop early if you're having trouble getting him to halt at a trot or slow cycle. You will both get frustrated as he would not submit to training.

Another element that influences a horse's ability to glide is the ground. On the improper surface, long slides do not occur. A hard, smooth base with two to three inches of loose earth on top makes for a fantastic sliding surface. Your horse will benefit from having a firm platform to glide on as a result, which will prevent his hooves from going too deep and minimise his glide time. It must be smooth to prevent your horse's foot from becoming stuck. This may cause your horse harm or shorten the slide.

Your feet's impact on the hard base will be lessened if there is loose, fluffy dirt on top of it. Your horse will be uncomfortable without this mat. When sliding, loose earth is easier for your horse to go through. Your horse won't glide very far if the top layer is too thick or too deep. To hold the slide in the dense, heavy earth, he also needs a lot of strength.

You can add rice husks or shavings to your sliding surface to make it better. The top layer will become fluffier and lighter as a result.

Your horse's capacity to slide may also be impacted by the shoes he is wearing. You have to wear a tempered flat bar iron slipper. Their width ranges from one inch to an inch and a half. They glide longer, and with less friction on the ground, the broader they are.

Since horseshoe nails are countersunk, the shoe and nail are flush. This lessens the friction. Similar to the beginning of a snowboard, the front quarter-inch of the shoe curls upward. By doing this, the horse will be able to slide without getting its toes trapped or caught on the ground. To facilitate easy dirt removal from the back, the rear of the shoe should run nearly straight back from the toe curve.

The shoe's trailer shouldn't go past the foot's bulb, but it also shouldn't reach back. The back foot needs to be trimmed, with the toes being slightly longer and the heel being lower than normal. This is done in order to increase the hoof's surface area and glide potential. Additionally, it lessens the possibility that the horse's toes will become entangled in the muck, which could cause him to receive bruises and injuries up to his middle knuckles. While these minor adjustments are welcome, don't let the impression that MORE is preferable. If the heel is trimmed very high, the horse may stoop and strain the tendon while attempting to stop. If you cut the heel too short, your hamstring may get strained.

Another crucial factor is the horse's size. Straight hind legs and forward-pointing feet are characteristics of horses with a higher gliding advantage. They can glide with their feet staying together. The horse's hind toes, however, spread outward as it enters the chute; the longer the chute, the more the rear legs will stretch. To put his feet back together, he needed to exit the slide.

A horse will slide in a V form if it has this issue. Horse owners can fix this by slightly rotating the horseshoe so that it points straight ahead. Swinging the toes slightly toward the inside of the foot also helps.

The most crucial element in deciding how long the slide is is how quickly the horse stops running. For instance, you would begin at a leisurely pace and progressively pick up the pace with each stride until you signalled for your horse to stop if you wanted them to perform a sliding stop across the entire arena floor.

You have to request to halt when the horse is moving quickly. Your horse will elevate his shoulders and extend his back feet when he accelerates. These two elements are essential building blocks for a successful long skate.

Be sure to properly time his acceleration. When you ask the horse to stop, you don't want it to go too quickly. He might disregard the stop signal if he moves too quickly. An instinctive horse will know how fast it can go and will still attempt to halt. Making him run faster will help him forget about the approaching stop and concentrate more on the running. He most likely lacks the strength to stop abruptly at a given pace, so, in essence, he won't try. You will need to do a great deal of trial and error to determine your horse's ideal running pace during extended breaks.

Recall that you shouldn't frequently ask your horse to come to a sudden stop at his fastest speed. He will become bitter if you do. Never forget to safeguard his foot locks when slipping by wearing non-slip footwear.

When you start to slow down as you get closer to stopping after accelerating your horse too quickly, it frequently results in a disappointing slide. There's no need to say it again; the horse is slowing down when you urge it to stop.

You have to stop the horse while it's running straight forward, never when it's turning or curving. The horse's body should also be straight, as if he were drawing an imaginary line from the tip of his nose to the end of his tail, and you urged him to stop. Your horse won't maintain his balance when you bring him to a stop if he has even a small bend in it, which could be hazardous for you both. Make sure he follows the arena straight, without turning or zigzagging, to guarantee a clean stop.

It matters much how the cyclist signals a stop. It takes precise timing and proper form to wield the reins properly so that your horse can glide across vast distances. It's crucial to know the proper strategy in addition to knowing what not to do.

Squeezing the reins tightly will make the slide go shorter rather than longer. Pulling too hard will cause your horse's hind legs to spread too far, and it will also force your boots into the ground too deeply to allow you to slip that far. A horse cannot maintain his balance by using his head or neck; he will not do so if the rider pulls on the reins abruptly.

To get this properly, there are three methods you can attempt. The first option might work, but you might need to try all three. There are three alternative approaches since each horse reacts differently. It will be up to you to figure out what method suits you and your horse the best.

The ideal response when your horse stops to slide down is to say, "Wow!" while maintaining a slack rein. This demonstrates that your horse will not interfere with the rider; thus, the longer he slips, the better. Just keep in mind to push lightly rather than pull. He can slip anywhere he pleases, unaffected by the reins. Your horse needs to halt and enjoy the glide for this strategy to be effective. This is probably how the typical horse will always come to a stop.

8. The Impact of the Rider on the Horse

Treating a horse like an inanimate thing, like a bicycle, is a common mistake made by novice riders. People are unaware of the sensitivity a horse has to both his environment and his rider. Honestly, before you even lay on his back, he might already know more about you than you think.

Before a frightened or ignorant rider even steps into the stirrup, some horses seem to possess an amazing capacity to identify her. This is the horse that only turns his butt over enough to prevent the rider from getting on, or he walks away from the mounting block. Because he is aware that his rider is unable to control or halt him, he is the horse who strides away from the other horses to the patch of green grass.

All a novice rider needs to do with these horses is project confidence and prepare a strategy before mounting. That may need asking for assistance from others, including having someone stand on the horse's offside to prevent him from shifting his butt or leaving before the rider has mounted. However, the green rider's awareness needs don't stop when he's in the saddle. Actually, a whole new set of variables emerges, like how he, namely his body, influences the horse in both positive and bad ways.

The horse's lips, back, and, for some, the sides of the barrel where the rider's knee rests are particularly sensitive. The horse may get uncomfortable and experience powerful, unpleasant effects from the rider's hands, even making the smallest contact with the bit through the reins. Certain horses have more sensitive backs than others, meaning that the horse will react to even the smallest change in the rider's seatbones. (Because highly trained dressage horses are taught to move off the rider's seat, they are extremely sensitive to even the smallest change in the hip or seat bone and will respond to the cue from the seat.)

But let's imagine the novice dressage rider from the horse's point of view rather than the experienced rider. Imagine the novice horseman beginning to trot. His hands fly up and down, his knees jiggle against the horse's sides, and he bounces wildly all over the horse's back, flopping like a fish. The poor horse is a picture of patience, stoically enduring this significant annoyance and insult to his sensitivities—he has no awareness he's doing these things.

What can a novice rider do to ease his mount's suffering, nevertheless, if they are not used to the horse's movements?

The rider must first recognise that his bouncing hands, flopping legs, and jiggling seat must all be under control. His hands ought to be lowered to the horse's withers to begin. He can prevent them from flying up and down if he places his hands on the withers so he can see where they are. To hold his hands there, he can even snag some mane between his fingers. That helps to relieve some of the horse's mouth pain. It's time to tackle the legs. The rider should focus on keeping his leg directly beneath his seat for support rather than jacking his legs out in front like he's sitting on a recumbent bicycle, which would cause his seat to flop further. He can imagine that his body is a tree, and his legs are its roots. He may consider lowering his knee and putting all of his weight into his heel. His legs may be now slightly more still against the horse's sides. The seat comes next.

It's a simple fact of nature that some horses have more bumps than others. In any case, the rider can sit properly to lessen his seat's bouncing on the horse's back and absorb the horse's bounce. The rider can stabilise his seat by maintaining his back straight, bending his lower back slightly to absorb the bounce, and continuing to press his knee into the ground while sinking his weight into his heel.

Controlling his own body and seat will become easier for the novice rider as soon as he obtains a sense of how the horse moves. He will be making good progress towards becoming a better, more sensitive, more feeling rider in the meantime if he continues to be conscious of how he affects his horse and seeks to lessen his impact on his steed!

Prioritising safety

I want to remind you that there is always a risk involved with anything involving horses, no matter how well-trained and experienced they are. It is astounding how some motorcyclists, out of sheer ignorance, make such serious blunders. If greater caution had been used, many incidents involving the riding and handling of horses could have been avoided.

For safety, never ride or jump without a quality hard hat.

It is not advisable to jump alone for safety reasons, and having someone on the ground to assist with installing poles, shifting fences, and other tasks is undoubtedly much more convenient.

When jumping, avoid using reins that are excessively long since your feet may become entangled in them.

To ensure that your foot slides out of the stirrup with ease in the event of a fall, wear heels at all times.

Should your saddle have a safety clip attached to the stirrup bar, make sure it can be readily flipped open or left free. This way, if you fall and your foot becomes trapped in the stirrup, the stirrup leather will slide out, and you won't be pulled.

Examine your horse's equipment on a regular basis, and replace or mend any damaged parts right away.

Pre-Purchase Interviewing Using The T.R.A.I.L.S. Method

The scoring methodology of T.R.A.I.L.S. is self-explanatory. The scoring sheet asks you for a score in each category and is self-explanatory. It should be possible for you to grab the scoring sheet, look it over for a minute, and start the scoring evaluation. The reasoning is the same whether you are using the scoring method for training or purchase; you will rate the horse as fairly as you can in each category.

There are 25 evaluation categories in the T.R.A.I.L.S. system. Thirteen evaluation categories in the "Ground Manners" part are assessed on a sliding scale from 0 to 5, with each category's score based on how important it is to the overall safety of the horse-human relationship. Twelve evaluation criteria are included in the "Under Saddle" section, and each category is assigned a score on a sliding scale (0–5 or 0–6) based on how crucial it is to the security and enjoyment of trail riding. There is a maximum score of 100. Since riding is the more significant of the two fundamental criteria, the scoring system is biased towards the horse's performance under saddle rather than its ground manners.

Furthermore, with practice, most ground manners can be quickly improved. Twenty-five of the chapters cover each of the testing topics in Part 4.

You'll read a synopsis of the exam, the value of trail riding, and some tips for raising your horse's performance. You will be able to rate the horse's performance for that task because there is sufficient space between score definitions. The horse's performance will occasionally fall into a grey area between two possibilities. For consistency, always go with the lowest of the two scores. A pre-purchase interview version of the T.R.A.I.L.S. test is provided below. To gain a better knowledge of the scoring process, you must go over the scoring chapters in Part 4.

The methodology will provide you with a qualitative way to recall each horse by summing the results for each category to get a total score. Additionally, it will allow you a way to compare the scores of the horses to assist you in deciding which ones to buy.

Don't worry if you're still a little confused—learning the categories and scoring system is really easy. You will be able to quickly learn how the system operates. Without any additional training, you should be able to use the scoring system below.

A score of 100 is flawless, although anything over 85 is regarded as remarkable. As of this writing, no horse has achieved a score of 100. If you choose to study each of the ensuing chapters before beginning your search, you will find them to be beneficial. The following chapters will also offer techniques for resolving behavioural problems and raising the T.R.A.I.L.S. score after you have bought your horse.

Before you buy the horse, you won't be able to score it in every category. But use the scoring sheet below and mark as many categories as you can. You should have enough information to leave the interview with enough clarity to help you distinguish between different horses in your mind.

Horse Nutrition Needs

We'll talk about what to feed horses in this section so they can get the food they need to meet their nutritional needs.

Gathers

This constitutes a sizable component of a horse's diet and contains grasses or legumes. The precise nutritional makeup of forages is hard to estimate because it tends to change depending on the grasses' maturity, the surrounding environment, and how the forages are managed. The precise nutritional makeup of forages may only be ascertained by a thorough laboratory investigation. The discussion of the many horse feed varieties in this area follows.

Legumes

Protein makes up a large component of the content of legumes. They are also a good source of calcium and other minerals. Legumes need ideal growth circumstances, such as good soil and mild weather, to offer the necessary nutrients. The two most common legumes fed to horses are clover and lucerne.

Hey

This is a reference to forages that are collected, dried, and then fed to horses. Legumes such as fescue, bluegrass, orchard grass, or timothy can contain it. Though they are typically more expensive, legume hay has a higher protein content than grass. Grass hays are more nutrient-dense when cut early in the growing stage, and they have longer leaves and stems than legumes. A healthy appearance is one of the primary markers of good nutrition in the hay; however, it is not a guarantee of quality. For this reason, don't give your horse hay that has mould or dust on it.

focuses

Concentrate feed is defined by the Association of American Feed Control Officials (AAFCO) as feed that is combined with another feed to enhance the overall feed's nutritional balance. A concentrate is usually meant to be combined with additional dilution or mixing to create a full feed. Forages and hay are the most popular natural sources of nourishment for horses. Still, manufacturers advocate mixing specially-made concentrates with other feed ingredients to provide specific nutrients like protein, carbs, and vitamins.

Grains

These comprise yet another group of chemicals fed to horses. You can feed grains by themselves or together with concentrate feed. A detailed list of some of the most widely used grains for horse feeding may be seen below.

Muesli Arguably, the most common gain fed to horses is this one. But oats cost a pretty penny. Although it has a lower digestible energy value than most other grains, it is usually high in fibre. Oats are also easier for equines to digest and are more pleasant to horses than most cereals.

Corn is another common grain that is fed to horses. On average, it has less fibre but twice as much digestible calorie value. Your horses should only be fed the appropriate amount of maize. Corn is tasty and simple to overfeed due to its high energy content, which can result in obesity. Mouldy maize can be fatal to horses, so you should never feed it to them.

Milo sorghum: This grain is low in fibre and rich in energy for feeding horses. Usually found as a small, hard kernel that needs to be treated in order to be digested effectively and made palatable for feeding horses. Since sorghum is almost never edible by itself, it is usually combined with other grains.

Barley Barley is a tasty grain that is suitable for feeding horses and has a moderate energy and fibre level. Similar to sorghum, it needs to be processed in some way to make it more palatable.

Wheat: Wheat is a high-energy grain that horses can consume, but because of its expensive cost, it is rarely used as feed. It needs to be processed for easier digestion and combined with other grains to make it more appealing because it also contains hard kernels.

Addenda

Supplemental nutrition is not the primary feed ingredient. Rather, they are provided as a supplement or a substitute for nutrients that might not be present in sufficient amounts in your horse's usual diet. Horse nutrients come in a variety of forms.

Supplements with protein: Soybean meal is the most popular protein supplement. It has a high protein content and is usually taken to provide necessary amino acids. Additional examples of protein supplements are peanut meal and cottonseed meal. Regarding crude protein content, they are roughly 48% and 53%, respectively. Another tasty and nutrient-dense protein supplement is brewer's grain, which is a byproduct of making beer. Another popular application for brewer's grain is as a supplement for fat and vitamin B.

Supplements with Fat: Another way to increase the amount of fat in horse feed is by supplementing it with fat. The most popular fat supplement for feeding horses is vegetable oil. Another item that has gained popularity recently as a feed supplement is rice bran.

The Guidelines for Horse Feeding

Knowing what to feed your horse is not enough; there are fundamental guidelines and factors to take into account when feeding horses in order to guarantee the best possible outcomes for their health and nutrition. Your general understanding of horse care depends on your ability to comprehend these guidelines. Some of the most crucial points to keep in mind when feeding your horse are listed below.

Give Your Horse Plenty of Roughage to Eat

Roughage should provide the majority of your horse's daily calorie intake. Good quality hay or pasture legumes and grass are just enough and should be your horse's primary diet. However, grain can be provided as an extra source of nutrition. Roughage digestion is most suited for a horse's digestive tract. Make sure you always have an ample amount of roughage on hand, and give grains exclusively as supplemental feeding.

A horse will typically require one to two per cent of its body weight in roughage each day. Usually, grazing horses can eat for up to sixteen hours every day. If your horse spends the majority of the day in a stall, you can attempt to mimic this natural feeding routine by keeping hay out in front of them. This will keep its digestive system supplied with roughage.

Feed grain frequently but sparingly

As previously said, you shouldn't feed your horses primarily grain. Alternatively, you might feed them tiny portions of grains several times over the day. Giving horses big amounts of grain at one time is not as natural as feeding them small amounts of grain often. This improves digestion for your horse and yields far superior outcomes.

Modify the Feed and Schedules progressively.

If you are going to alter your horse's diet, it is best to do so gradually as opposed to all at once. Incidental alterations in the availability of nutrients can result in colic or founder. This also holds if you are adjusting the amount of feed you feed your horse. Don't make drastic changes to your diet plan at once; instead, make small adjustments over a few weeks. Replacing 25% of the current feed with a new meal every two days is an easy way to switch up your horse's diet. Keep an eye out for significant changes and negative consequences so you can modify as necessary.

Feed utilizing a precise and reliable feed measurement.

A crucial guideline for feeding horses is to make sure you give them a regular amount of grain at the right time each day. A thousand-pound horse will typically require fifteen to twenty pounds of hay each day. Hay is usually distributed in flakes; however, there can be a significant variation in the quantity of hay in each flake. Everything is dependent upon the size of the type of hay and flakes. The amount of hay you want to give your horse should be measured out, and you should only give them what they actually require.

Feeding your horse right before or after exercise is not recommended.

As energetic creatures, horses engage in a variety of physical activities every day. If you intend to ride your horse after it has done eating, give it at least an hour to finish. A three- or four-hour delay is advised for even more demanding activity. Additionally, wait until your horse has completely recovered from work before feeding them. Your horse will find activity much more difficult if they have a full stomach since their lungs, which are vital for any strenuous physical exercises, will have less area to expand. Additionally, blood flow to the digestive system's organs will be redirected during strenuous exercises, which may slow down gut motility.

Educating Your Foal To Take Charge

When you are satisfied that he is starting to relax, progressively attach a harness. I usually use a rope harness for foals—no clasps!

Every rope harness is perfect. Deb and her Arab Colt are models.

To progressively scoop his nose, place one arm over his neck and pass the bridle's end beneath his neck. Although you are risking frightening your foal, try not to go flicking it excessively as you may on your more experienced pony (I see this a lot!). After you've scooped the nose, tie your bridle high and securely beneath the neck, but avoid getting too near because that will obviously stop him from breathing.

After you have your harness in place, move aside, grasp his head gently, and walk over to his hip. He starts driving by moving his hip. Push his hip to first gain a small advance from the rump if that's what you want to do. In response to his advancement, apply pressure to his hip and lead rope, and offer assistance by lowering your hands to your sides and maintaining a loose posture. (For definitions of "alleviation" and "splashing time," see the glossary.)

Taking the lead. Model: Pearl, a fantastic dog barrel horse today!

Give him ten or fifteen seconds to process and think about what you're asking for. Try not to look at him during that pouring ten or fifteen seconds; instead, turn away or towards the ground.

After a few repetitions of a similar cycle on a comparable side with stress on the lead rope and centre or a push on the hip to obtain a stage or two from the rump, assist.

Flip to the other side and recapitulate the exchange. It might take less time, even if you have to start over from scratch on the other side. As long as you receive a stage or two from each side, it doesn't matter whose side you begin on. Proceed to move four or more times from one side to the next.

The next step is to walk a step or two to the hip, after which you should go out to the side to start the front. Squeeze his hip slightly while applying minimal pressure to the strap lead. At that moment, go backwards and face your foal directly.

By pushing your foal to one side, you are essentially giving him a little reeling. Give relief as soon as you observe him shift his shoulder to come closer to you or take a step. This is your place of business. After you've given him a good soaking time of ten or fifteen seconds, repeat it. In the future, give him a moment's assistance by dropping your hands and turning away, and tug the lead rope immovably but gently until he moves his leg or even twists his knee.

After that, relieve him by pulling on the lead line from the side until he takes a step. Immediate relief is akin to an immediate reward. Keep trading to both sides, switching between moving the front and rear for one or two stages. We can ask him to lead once you have one or two stages from the front and the rear on both the left and right flanks.

Push his rump for a stage, starting at the rump. Then, go back away from the side and tug on the lead rope to make the front follow and travel with you. Try to drive the hindquarters and then the front in a single fluid motion. When you've done so, step back and pull the lead rope.

Getting the hindquarter moving first or disengaging the hindquarter and then stepping aside to move the front is, in my experience, the most effective approach to teach your foal to release pressure.

Once he has taken a step or two and has been following you for a few steps, challenge his advances by taking a step or two yourself. Assist if he follows!

2. Horse Sensitivity

Humans and horses have different perspectives on and experiences of the world.

2-1: Observatory

Form of the lens:

Compared to the lens of a human eye, the lens of a horse eye is less flexible. The vision of horses is more like seeing through a trifocal lens. A trifocal lens allows for close-up focus in one area, mid-distance focus in another, and distance focus in a third.

This explains why horses' heads need to be in such a position to see clearly. They must tilt their head upward for greater vision in the distance and downward for a closer look at objects.

A horse's field of vision is greatly limited when he is forced to maintain his nose straight above the ground. You may easily give this a try. Observe your field of vision while standing with your head raised. Next, droop your head until your nose is pointing downward. Right now, note your field of vision.

Limiting a prey animal's field of vision by making it require vertical bending can result in severe mental stress and detrimental muscle strain, as the animal relies on early danger detection and flight response for survival.

Set on the side of the head are the eyes:

Horse eyes function more independently than human eyes because they are located on either side of a huge head. The horse's binocular vision—the ability to focus on something in front with both eyes—is restricted to a triangle in front due to the way its eyes are positioned.

His field of vision with binoculars goes beyond the three feet straight in front of him due to the blind area caused by his nose shape when his head is straight.

In addition to his forward binocular vision, the horse's eyes can see nearly 180 degrees from side to side and back, much like an automobile's rearview mirror.

Figure 3: When a horse's head is up or down, he can see about 180 degrees on either side.

Although it is not as precise as binocular vision, side or peripheral vision is quite good at detecting motion.

For this reason, when horses are startled by anything moving, they frequently leap sideways at first, then spin to face the motion's source in order to have a better view.

The horse's mind is preoccupied and not connected to his peripheral vision when he is using his binoculars to look intently forward. This helps to explain why we should approach horses cautiously from the side or rear, as they may be truly startled by activity behind them if they are focused on something in front of them.

Horses appear to be able to sleep with their eyes open as well. If a horse appears extremely laid back, with a cocked hip, relaxed ears, a low head, and a floppy bottom lip, it's possible that he's too sleepy to notice us approaching, even though his eyes are open. Giving the horse a warning "nicker" or uttering a few words when approaching always pays off.

Light Strength:

As long as there is some light in the surroundings, horses' enormous eyes allow them to see very well at night. I can personally attest to this because, while on a sunset ride, I was stranded on the far side of a hydroelectric river when water abruptly burst from the dam upstream. To get to the dam and cross over to our home side, we had to ride on an unidentified track in complete darkness.

Horse eyes adjust from light to dark and from dark to light more slowly than human eyes do. When moving a horse from a dark building into bright sunlight or from sunlight into a dark vehicle or trailer, it's critical to keep this in mind. While his vision adjusts, we should let him stand with his head in the door.

Horses have a triangle-shaped blind area that extends around one metre in front of their nose. For this reason, when they get up close to examine anything, they must droop their head.

By positioning your hands, as shown in the image below, you can approximate what it would be like to have a long snout like a horse. Take note of how it impacts your vision directly in front of your nose.

In the two years that Josie and her mother lived in Oregon, they only made one visit to Aunt Sue's house.

Her mother had stated, "Driving out there is too expensive." However, Josie would now be residing in this region of high desert. For a twelve-year-old orphan, what was ahead?

Finally, Aunt Sue turned onto the house's gravel driveway. The empty corral caught Josie's attention right away.

Aunt Sue's son Jack used to own a horse. It had been years since the corral and barn had been unoccupied. Josie observed the natural bunch of grass growing in the spaces between the boulders. Made of strong posts, cross rails, and wire fencing, the corral fence appeared to be in good shape.

A fleeting excitement surged through Josie. Could she get a horse and tack it in the corral if she lived here?

Josie waved the thought away in a hurry. She was now an orphan, and horses were expensive. How on earth was she going to buy a horse?

She noticed the house as they went by the barn. It wasn't an apartment or a duplex; it was a real house. Although it seemed unpretentious, the two-story home was pristine. Additionally, Aunt Sue had allowed her to remain in Jack's room. It would be her room.

Josie recalled how she had looked into Jack's room on the one visit she and her mother had taken when they initially relocated to Oregon. Numerous horse-related posters and photos adorned the walls. Were they still present?

When she visited, Jack had already moved out. He had enlisted in the Marines and was currently serving in a distant nation, waging war. However, his room had been tidy and orderly, as though he would return at any moment.

Josie supposed she could live comfortably in his room if the pictures and posters were still up on the walls. Several photos of horses would soothe her hurting heart.

She then gave her mother some thought. She would never see her mother again. She is never going to be able to share her dreams or laugh with her in the future.

Josie's mother had also cherished horses. She had consistently assured Josie that "someday" they would have enough cash to purchase a home and a horse. Josie would be able to ride her horse all summer long, she had promised—someday.

When sprinting to the first barrel, glance at a point on the fence: NEVER DO THIS. The area on the fence will no longer be in the right location when your horse approaches the barrel. The direction you want your horse to follow should be clearly visible to you. Instead, stare twenty to thirty feet ahead of you, past your horse's ears, to the area of the ground where you want him to run, all the while keeping the barrel in your line of sight. You and your horse will both reach the barrel more quickly and easily if you do this. Although your horse cannot see where you are looking, he can read body language, and if he perceives you to be staring off into the distance, he will likely not assess the barrel accurately.

Glancing to the next barrel, I repeat, NEVER DO THIS. Always focus only on your destination. Aim your gaze twenty to thirty feet ahead of you via your horse's ears. After you have completed your turn, keep the following barrel in your direct line of sight. Before you finish your turn, you actually shift your body weight sufficiently such that your horse must change his stride in order to maintain his balance. Usually, this change puts your horse squarely into the barrel.

Taking a horse's breath away: NEVER DO THIS. You will only cause your horse's lungs to become devoid of air by lunging as hard as you can. Instead of kicking your horse with your legs, use them to push him. Remain seated while applying pressure to your calves or spurs. Never allow your knees to leave your horse's side or your butt to come out of the saddle. Always land a kick with your knees first. Huge flapping kicks and allowing your butt to come out of the saddle will just make your horse unbalanced, causing him to slow down in an attempt to make up for it.

Never, ever whip your horse at every step on the way home. Because it takes a horse at least one stride to adjust, he is unable to react to the initial strike. Before you repeat any command, you must give him time to react. You are merely giving him a thrashing if you just keep hitting him. Your horse will typically refuse to return to the arena if you don't give him enough time to react. Squeezing your horse's heels or spurs with your legs is the finest technique to motivate him to finish hard and finish the race all the way home. You can be sure he'll react if you have spurs on, even bumper spurs. If this is still insufficient to persuade your horse to race to the finish, give him a couple of shoulder slaps. Use an over and under, a quirt, or a whip if a slap isn't enough to prick your horse. Any of these can be used, but only once or twice during your run home. Make sure you give him a step or two in between swats so he can react to you swatting him. It shouldn't be necessary for you to always employ a whip. I almost never need to use the quirt that I always wear on my wrist when I run. On the other hand, I can fix the issue immediately if I sense my horse cheating on me as we're running home. The next time, all I have to do is lift my arm and threaten to have him push all the way home because he will remember it.

Never put too much weight into your stirrups too quickly. You can use this signal to alert your horse when you're ready to enter the arena for your barrel run. In order to get ready for his race, your horse will begin to increase his adrenaline. If you place your weight in the stirrups too soon, he will become anxious and wash out. I'm not sure if he will have to make his run now or later. You may assist your horse in resting until it's time for his run by avoiding putting your weight in your stirrups until you're ready to enter the arena. This way, your horse won't get washed out.

Asking your horse to enter the arena while holding the reins too tightly drawn up is something you should never do. Your horse will grow confused and anxious at the gate as a result of this. Issues with the gate can arise when you give mixed signals with your reins. You must be prepared when you approach the gate. Keep your reins tight, but only apply a small amount of pressure to your horse's head. Make sure to release all bits of pressure when you're ready for him to go on his run.

www.ingramcontent.com/pod-product-compliance
Lightning Source LLC
Chambersburg PA
CBHW052152110526
44591CB00012B/1956